Jiří Orten

Selected poems

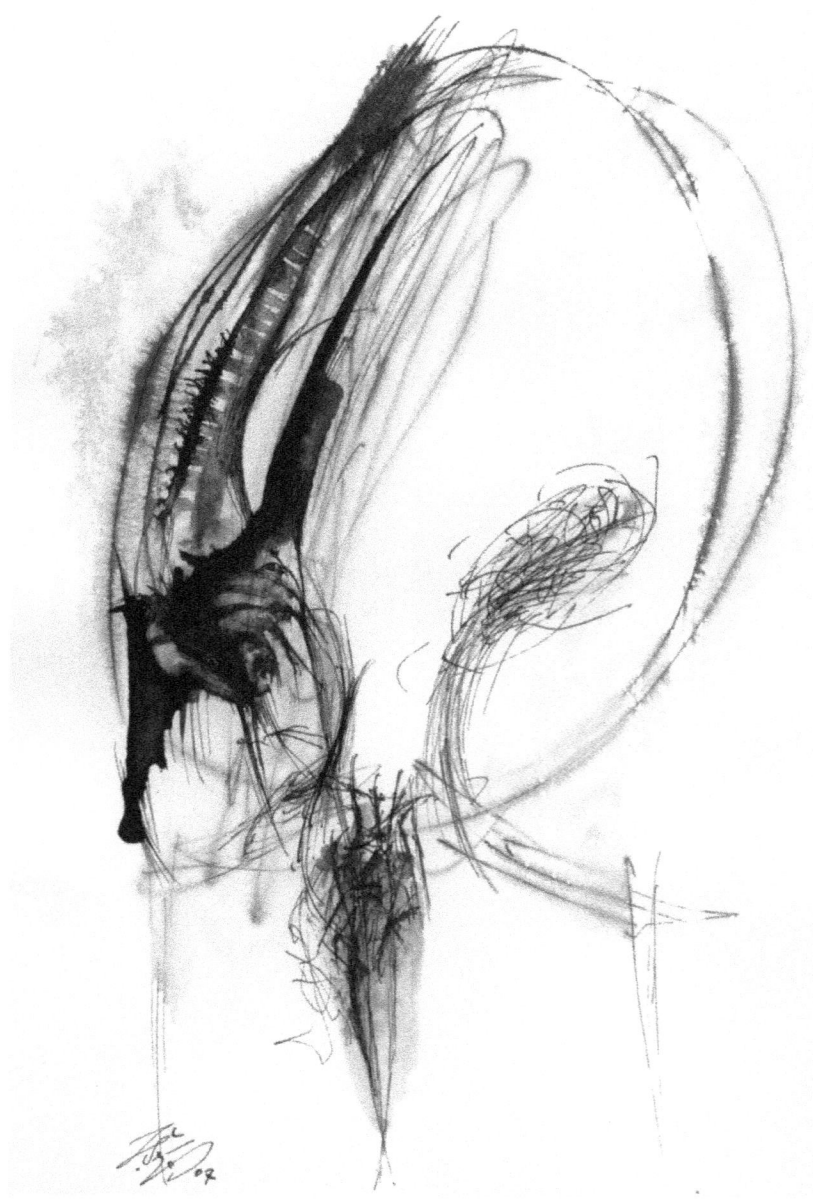

Jiří Orten

Selected poems

Translated by Josef Tomáš
Edited by Betty Boyd

Melbourne 2007

Published 2008 by arima publishing

www.arimapublishing.com

ISBN 978-1-84549-288-5

Printed and bound in the United Kingdom

Typeset in Palatino 12/16

arima publishing
ASK House, Northgate Avenue
Bury St Edmunds, Suffolk IP32 6BB
t: (+44) 01284 700321

www.arimapublishing.com

*This translation has been kindly subsidised by the
Ministry of Culture of the Czech Republic.*

Cover and Illustrations

Jaroslav Šerých, born 1928. Czech painter, illustrator, sculptor and mosaicist. In 1948-49 he studied copper-engraving at the School of Applied Arts in Jablonec nad Nisou and in 1948-50 at the school of Jewellery Design in Turnov. In 1950 he was accepted by the Academy of Fine Arts in Prague and completed his studies in the studio of Vladimír Pukl in 1955. In these early years he showed equal ability in painting, colour lithography and book illustration. He first exhibited in group shows with the group M 57. He also undertook study trips to various major cities in Europe. His early paintings, such as the *Distant Swan* (1952) were influenced by Symbolism, while oils and pastels done in 1954-55 were mainly lyrical portraits. His intense and long-lasting interest in the effect of light resulted in his move to non-figurative work in 1958-59. His first paintings in this manner were lyrical abstracts that showed a deliberate relationship to the work of Zao-Wou-Ki. These were followed by various forms of informal painting and graphic art until 1969. Šerých did not, like many artists, revert to figuration when the trend toward abstraction had ebbed: rather, abstract and figurative work alternated in his output, each deriving from strands in his artistic personality. In this somewhat uneasy synthesis he drew strength from a consistently spiritual conception of the world and art, though both his abstract and figurative paintings of the years 1960-75 are meditative rather than religious. In 1975 with the painting *Evening in the garden*, Šerých turned to biblical subject-matter, confirming his status as one of the most original and distinguished figures in the Czech painting of his era. From 1976 he worked on plaques in copper and coloured enamel, in high relief; he also illustrated children's books, worked in mosaic and painted large murals (e.g. *Man and Metal*; in East Slovac Iron Works, Kosice).

Oxford University Press, 2003

Contents

Foreword 9

What is called a poem 15

A gilded vision 16

Oh you gaping eyes 17

Little feast 18

A sad confession 19

An unnamable poem 20

A little girl on a walk 21

What melancholy knows 22

My deer, my little deer 23

The drowned one 24

For a kiss I'm too small 25

A look back 26

Waiting 27

Happy quarters 28

November 30

Such a sad day 31

A prayer 32

Merrily, merrily 33

A little answer to a great Why 35

Early spring 36

A poem of dusk 38

A little stone 40

That land 43

I've met a fountain 46

Poem of new glory 47

A lost soldier 49

To whom do I belong? 51

The unborn one 52

The unwritten one...53

Wild radish 54

The first poem..55

Sunset..57

A summer poem..59

Job's words are closing...61

A raw youth 62

A poem of hope..63

The wounded..64

What a canary told me 65

My answer to the canary..66

The lamentations of Jeremiah................................67

After the music 73

A ride 74

The first prayer...75

It's warm close to you 76

The second prayer...78

Red painting 79

A lea 81

The Christmas poem..82

The third elegy 83

The third prayer 86

Girl's song 87

The seventh elegy..88

The eighth elegy 93

A hangover 97

Night and day...98

The moist one 99

Autumn 100

My trees of years 101

Translator's Note.. 102

Foreword

The Czech poet, Jiří Orten, started writing at the age of nine years. In 1939, he wrote: "I want to be a poet with all my heart. With all my heart and, even more, I want to die for it." He sent these words to the poet František Halas, who published Orten's first book of poetry *The First Reader Spring* under the pseudonym Karel Jílek, because Orten, being a Jew, could not be published under his own name.

In the same year, Orten's older brother Ota Ornest emigrated to London. He asked Jiří to join him, in order to escape certain deportation to a concentration camp, but Jiří declined, not only because he was in love with a girl, but also because he felt that he was incapable of writing in his mother language in any other country.

On the 30th August 1941, the day of his twenty-second birthday, he was knocked down by a German ambulance in one of streets of Prague. Because he was a Jew, he was refused first-aid treatment in a near-by hospital. He died two days later of a brain haemorrhage in the Jewish ward of another hospital. Thus his prophetic words in the letter to Halas came true.

Orten's mother Berta and his younger brother Zdeněk were deported to the ghetto of Terezin. In autumn 1944, fifteen year old Zdeněk was transported to Auschwitz.

By some miracle both he and his mother survived the war.

Despite dying so young, Orten left behind a large body of work and lived to see the publication of two more books of his poetry. In 1940, he published *The Journey Towards Frost* under the pseudonym Karel Jílek, and, a short time before his death, his third book *Wild Radish* was published under the pseudonym Jiří Jakub. Under the same pseudonym, his friend Zdeněk Urbánek published Orten's extensive poem *The Lamentations of Jeremiah* in the 1941 annual almanac. In this composition, the verse "I'm that land of Night" is repeated many times, aiming to evoke not only the loss of The Promised Land, but also our fatherland, which was enslaved by Nazis.

Orten was not published again during the war, because it was revealed that his pseudonyms were hiding a Jew, and anyone publishing Jewish authors was threatened with death. Not until the end of the war could his last two poetry books be published: *Lead Astray* and *Elegies*.

Orten wrote almost every day and the books contain all his poems, daily records, dreams, reflections and citations from the writings of the authors he loved. His note from the 27th October 1940 is worth citing, in order to understand the circumstances under which he lived and wrote: "I am prohibited from :

- leaving the house after eight o'clock in the evening;
- renting an apartment by myself;
- visiting cafes, wine-bars, pubs, cinemas, theatres, concerts, apart from one or two cafes specifically designated for me;
- going to parks and gardens;
- going to municipal woods;
- travelling outside the Prague city limits, so I cannot visit my mother in Kutná Hora;
- shopping in any stores except between 11 a.m. and 1 p.m. and between 3 p.m. and 5 p.m.;
- acting in a play or taking part in any other public activity;
- belonging to any association;
- going to any school;
- having any social contact with ordinary Czechs, and they are prohibited from associating with me. They may not greet me nor stop to talk to me except about essential matters (e.g. while shopping, etc.)."

After the communist take-over in February 1948, all publications of Orten's poetry were again banished in Czechoslovakia, his work being condemned as "degenerative sludge." Only the unremitting courage and perseverance of Orten's admirers forced the publication of his diaries in 1958 and again, ten years later, during the Prague Spring in 1968. Unfortunately, this was followed by another communist "dark age" of some twenty years.

Only after the totalitarian regime had fully collapsed, in 1989, could the full greatness of the poet be re-introduced to the Czech community, and his work repeatedly published in subsequent years.

In my edition of Orten's work – so far seven volumes have been published from the planned nine – three of his books are truly unique: *The Blue Book, The Striped Book* and *The Red Book*, written from autumn 1938 until the eve of his death in 1941, concluded by the poem *My Trees of Years*.

His friend, the pianist Líza Kleinová, who witnessed Orten's fatal injury, entrusted me with an extraordinary story. In summer 1941, about one month before his death, they were strolling along the Vyšehrad ramparts, when he was captivated by a girl, who was completely immersed in reading a slim book. Orten managed to get closer to see what the girl was reading. He discovered that the book contained poems of the Czech poet Jiří Wolker, who died at the age of twenty-four years, in 1924. Orten said wistfully to Liza: "Do you think that, one day, some girls will read my verses?"

Orten's wish has been fulfilled to the last detail. I am one of many such girls who indeed read his verses. 2008 will be the 16th anniversary of Orten's Poetry Festival in his birthplace Kutná Hora. As part of the festival, a competition is held between poets younger than twenty-two years of age. So far over 3,000 young poets have competed for prizes and honours. An almanac is published every year, together with the first-fruits of the most successful author.

We leave our pilgrimage through Orten's work with the closing verse of the poem *To the Silenced One,* written by František Halas soon after Orten's death: "At the time when fish will swim in the cathedrals, this poet will be called on by his name."

Marie Rút Křížková, 4/12/2007.

What is called a poem

What is called a poem
is this what you still want?
To sob cloistered and solemn
and yet still love a lot?

Hear the tick-tock! It's *Him*!
A play that has no hope
What is called a poem
is this what you still want?

You know that many times
words sound extremely odd
God keeps our mouths tight locked
when He can't give good rhymes

What is called a poem
is this what you still want?

A gilded vision

A gilded vision wants all things to race
while darkness permeates and drinks night's breeze
Who sleeps alone yearns for his mother's embrace
when low-voiced longing whispers in his ears

Listen my friend the clouds were in full climb
and I allured by soft dampness of lips
felt like a cherub who stole bits of time
and hid them away to keep a few sips

of it Look out! His breath is nearly spent
when air runs out in this abandoned room
A gilded vision – no hurry to end –
is mixing pure joy with my recent gloom

Oh you gaping eyes

Oh you gaping eyes oh eyes behind eyes
you others whose soft look does not entice
you cousins of faith from light far afield
you for whom the balm is what can't be healed
you spies on lovers with little to toy
you evermore bewailing any joy
you taken by death long before your birth
you running away from girls and poems
you leaf-shaped and friendly clairvoyants
finding the secret door to new parlance

Oh you gaping eyes oh eyes behind eyes
through you to see through you to surmise
the lover's breast as a dream undeterred
you determined never to say a word
you for ever resolved not to descry
you only you the apple of my eye
you knowing so well and God knows as well
about one heart which has been starved to hell
that starvation is like eternal ice
oh you gaping eyes oh eyes behind eyes

Little feast

A sugar bowl and a shoehorn
as slender as Little Red Riding Hood's heel
a sugar bowl and a shoehorn
on this desk smooth and timeworn
with just one wine-spilled tear

Oh who might have drunk this tear
who drank it before he let it spill
did he wipe his lips dry and clear
did he hide another one somewhere here
the other one that I feel

A sad confession

The most pristine light is always at dawn
and yet it must come this minuscule while:
my face fades out for you with all my hope
when even from under your lids it goes

Because my heart does not know how to fly
knows only how to walk on its tiptoes
one ev'ning it pitter-patters to fawn
and you find my hand on an envelope

Then you say that it is with great regret
that darkness is most beautiful at dusk
and suddenly you look quite old and gray

Then you cry when you have received a word
from my look well hidden under my mask
and you'll be glad that love is here to stay

An unnameable poem

Oh barrel-organs in calm of calms
a wound in wounds so well disguised
oh stifled breath that has no qualms
a corner piece never baptized

Oh cold in fingers full of lust
a shelter in someone's hiding place
oh love in women's deep disgust
oh ugliness of utmost grace

You the thawed ice in summer time
a taint on all my happiness
you my flight which failed its climb
oh the vigil for the one who sleeps

you fraternize without a fight
with all kinds of hearts eye to eye
you give what's to give with delight
to girls who are blind and shy

A little girl on a walk

We walk everywhere and ask everyone
if they've seen a girl picking up berries
Who asks too much will learn nothing and none
may even pierce himself with shoes undone
so he won't find her when she disappears

A finch composed a song so much refined
if not he it's one of the other birds
I lean from my window and try to find
what she may like but nothing comes to mind
The Jolly Ploughman overturned my words

Cloudlets above me turn to nemesis
A shade of red hue that is shown by some
is my anxious heart beating with unease
she went away and might not hear its pleas
nor see that I was giving her a sign

Then when exhausted she silently bends
and suddenly quickly becomes astir
when she has learned that I'm in all her scents
and even in the trees with all those birds
and in a deaf nettle waiting for her

What melancholy knows

In the pause between life and what is there
a little tomcat in the pond alone
sleeps on the floor with fishes and a stone
and it's not coming there it always has time
Can you see him? he thinks he will return

It's called a weight that they tied to his neck
while the moon that he loved so much somehow
looks into the water taken aback
that he is not greeted by his miaow
because his eyes are turned elsewhere

And he drinks slowly as if hiding his guilt
for all the goldfinches he caught and killed
for all the eaves he ran along with rain
and all the lady-cats he won't see again

In the pause between life and what is there
sleep comes slowly as when going to bed
at dawn when you'd wish to sleep in your lair
for ever with no thought of coming back

My deer, my little deer

My deer my little deer
where is your hind?
my deer my little deer
your mother why is she not here?

A shot through your brow now bleeds
and leaves you blind

You should know you lover of trees
who used to strip the bark of birches bare
and soon their sweet sap made you drunk again
that your wounded head can't carry your pain
which is sinking into dead leaves
all fours up in the air

The drowned one

For the face of your warmth
you flew along every brook
between banks you have lost
to dark lands you mistook
for the face of your warmth

Unseen and troublesome
you've been grasping the ground
at the bottom with awesome
darkness floating around
unseen and troublesome

Lovers hide behind parapets
where unknown is the face of grace
smashed by that which they took by stealth
from mortal beauty of poor waves

But one hears you gave it all
to shivering water-sprites
just by opening your thighs

Love's pittance even so small
assists you to bear death's toll

For a kiss, I'm too small

For a kiss, I'm too small,
said a hare to the grass,
when he ran to its sprawl.
My years are running on,
said a hare to the grass,

this morning I won't miss,
from afar I have called,
this good morn I won't miss.
I won't give you a kiss,
for a kiss I'm too small,

my years are running on,
soon they will be bygone,
said a hare to the grass.
My years are running on,
so wildly on and on,

I'd love to catch them up
before the darkness nears,
said a hare to the grass.
I'd love to catch them up.
And he pricked up his ears.

A look back

Oh rains, brought to humming by quietude!
Without you the trees in the woods look black.
Why does the wind not bring you back
to wake my body from its jaded mood?

How wonderful to stand there unconcerned
of water, drenched from head to toe,
allowing its droplets to button up my coat,
and, with heavy eye-lids, to listen how it rained!

Then, during the rumble of raining bits,
when, from their nests, young crows fell out,
there ran to them a rain-soaked ant
and greeted them with its antennae-tips.

Waiting

Czech lands behind the panes of sad souls
my horizon I see you well
from within my grief as the most pure
deep down where the depth of lakes allure
Czech lands behind the panes of sad souls
on huntsman's watch to no avail

to be full of laughter for one's past
with all that tears have for a smile
to know that love is fond of torment
before you receive its full consent
to know that a song can only last
if it can prove that it's worthwhile

Just a hint before I become numb
to words for the rest of my day:
who's still alive can climb a mountain
and one must think of Jack-o'-lantern
and Tattercoat and Hop-o'-my-thumb
that they too sometimes went astray

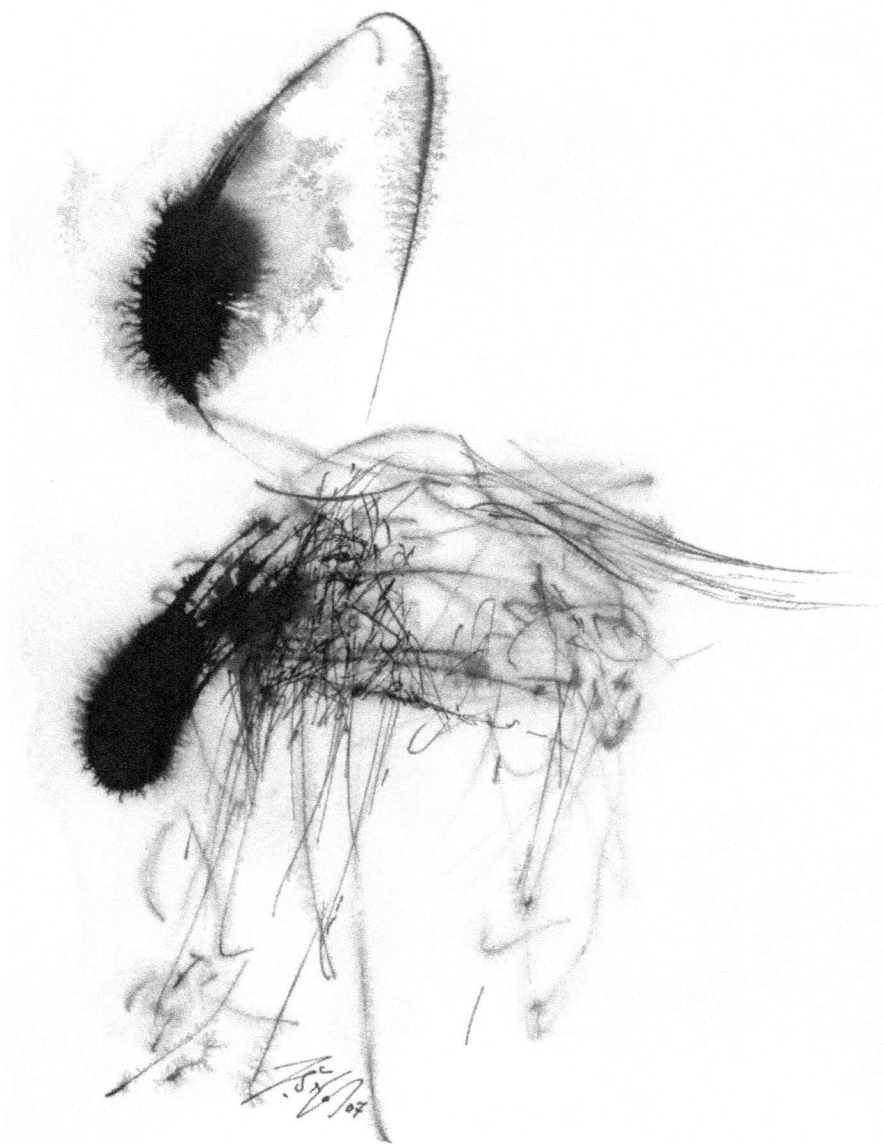

Happy quarters

You, happy quarters, quarters of silence,
where do you end, whither your end may end?
You are like life in a breathless cadence,
where one is waiting for one's belov'd friend.

She's coming and wants something to mention
from the secret the loom of her head weaves,
and, as ev'ry authentic magician,
she hid in her sleeves.

You cannot guess until she moves to leave.
Then the truth slowly sets in:
the wise girl has nothing else to give
for, already, she gave you everything.

November

Once upon a time, the time that goes by
like your tears, like wants, too small to remember,
an old gentleman comes, his neck awry:
What have you lost and sought, my poor November?

A wreath of steam, when cold winter sucks away
a snowed-up park, with all its trees and stones,
and needles of rain that began to wail
on broken and asthmatic gramophones.

What's played? Some magic from a worn out score,
from the leaves that fell on roads with no camber,
while girls sleep in caves where dragons snore.
You've lost! You won't find! Oh, my poor November!

Such a sad day

Dedicated to Jiří Klan

Such a sad day, like many in each year,
it whirls with clouds and a barber's pole.
Soon I'll depart, for Christmas is quite near,
to touch on joy and warm my benumbed soul.

A letter arrives, so my friend still lives,
my dear friend, my brother, who looks like me.
I dare to say: stop with your moody drifts,
there's something sadder that this day may see.

Don't you know what it is? It walks around
all waters and they nurture it and praise.
Of course, a little rain which soaks the ground
with luck, love and a coffin on a hearse.

A prayer

A graveyard, old, with no cross, no fresh grave.
My very first grief:
so beautiful, so deep in me engraved
by stones, grasses, silence and ignorance.
My Lord, let me run after it at once!
Why have you bound my feet?

A bookshop, an arcade and a white fount,
that's the way up to St. Barbara's dome,
so slim and tall, it makes my blood run out.
The Virgin of miners and sextons' frocks
silently sprouts in my heart, and unlocks
stony Kuttenberg, the secret in stone.

Seven times locked and bolted is her home.
So oft I knocked, but ev'ry time in vain.
Oh earth, oh earth, oh earth, you are alone,
and I wanted so much to run and feel
that I still have you, as you have me still,
that we aren't alone, but together again …

Merrily, merrily

You've lost me, my God, and what took your place?
Of you, who mustn't dream since well endowed.
That silly Lot! He didn't turn his face.
The valiant valour has cut its own shroud.

Look for me, so long as I can be found!
I'm drained like all that's overgrown with weeds,
in coils and hoops, with corners all around,
a senseless bed (for there's no Procrustes).

For there's no Procrustes! All that might've been
is now no more! (It dwells in heaven's nooks!)
A crack-brained woodworm drills its work obscene
to the other side, through the Book of Books.

My death does not count; my wonderment does.
That stone, which weighs down my words and sounds:
a grave-stone, like all others with buzz and fuzz,
falling apart and dead, when once announced.

Merrily, merrily we've been announced.
Whereto those sounds and sighs and trembling grounds?
The way is dead, with monkeying entranced,
which already knows us inside and out.

I don't count! The future of ruins deigns
by filling itself in with night dawn's dust.
And the hands of God, which He changed to canes.
It's *His* salvation that leaves me nonplussed.

A little answer to a great Why

For the last rivulet, for all that shakes,
for cats and blackbirds, for the world that reels,
for beautiful walks and for basking snakes,
for love of the dead, for pain that never heals,

for a silky touch, a touch of the skin
that lures my fingers, then hurts their fingertips,
and dares my mouth to teach me how to win
with wine and sweet pancakes on soft white sheets,

for this lone hour, so quiet and old,
falling asleep, and wanting me to sleep,
for peaceful dreams, for music, great and bold,
for glory of the poor, let my life leap.

Early spring

While a bird chirrups high,
and the song still sticks in its throat,
I hear little bells, as they softly call:
rise up, grasses, wake up, you sleepy all,
from the earth to the sky!

How wonderful it is
to stretch up in the morn!
The rivers rose, clasping their hands, headstrong,
behind their head, the sea, where they slept so long –

where are you going, dawn?
I go to blue the sky,
to give the bells more voice for their soft fall:
rise up, grasses, wake up, you sleepy all,
wake up, flowers, and fly!

A vault

My ardour, silent under thick furs,
which keep away all cold.
Under that calm, it silently stirs.
To succumb? To whose fold?

A brother and friend are somewhere else.
And here, here in my midst,
solitude gives a nod, an empty purse.
No sound. A void. A darkened niche.

Speak up and wait till time becomes loose,
a very small time, nameless,
then a strange hand will give you a noose.
What is it? An echo? What else?!

A poem of dusk

The lilac garden has turned dark.
Oh, words in bloom, all scent and spark.

The sky is crying tears of brass,
reddish on daisies in the grass,

and, behind, on a shaded church,
the sky's crying, left in the lurch.

What is that scent that cools and fools?
All over the world, darkness rules.

All over the world, all is as here,
a sad garden can't hold its tear.

It looks through panes, giving no sound,
like a stem, bent down to the ground,

like the boxwood – my good old pal –
the snow-worm, the saddest snake of all.

And while I'm writing this rhymed note,
a star is asking why it's not

like dew, as red as coppered brass,
left by the sky on sleepy grass,

and, like my heart, and, like my words,
drunk by the songs of lyrebirds.

And it knows well why she so asks,
when it glimmers in glowing masks,

when it glimmers with glist'ning shine,
like my head, befuddled with wine.

A little stone

And he's called a pea.
Sometimes he'll roll,
for he can't do otherwise;
other times, behind a rock,
he'll play with a toy gunlock,
unsure if it's his role.
And he's called a pea,
and the gun jerks him up.

A rock? No! A pebble
or just the sun on it.
Such a silent aged tremble
weighs down my love a bit.

Four times at least,
I've come here already.
In a glen under trees,
steps in mud unsteady,
and in a fleeting green,
in leaves that often bleed,
where dead men's source had been,
you can, in silence, read.

Little stones. Four already!
And, instead of me, each one
tells how hard it is to steady

a habit hearts can't bring undone.

Sharper than knives,
like a wind on the lea,
like a wind on the lea.
My God, so many lives
he has, and he's called a pea,
and he lies there on a grave,
oh, my God, so many lives!

And now, he doesn't even roll!
Moss grows here all around,
hot and heavy in a hole,
he's unsure of his role.
Nobody would make a bet
that, very soon, he'll forget
it was you who had burned out.
My God, he'd love to be as light
as a breath or a plumelet.

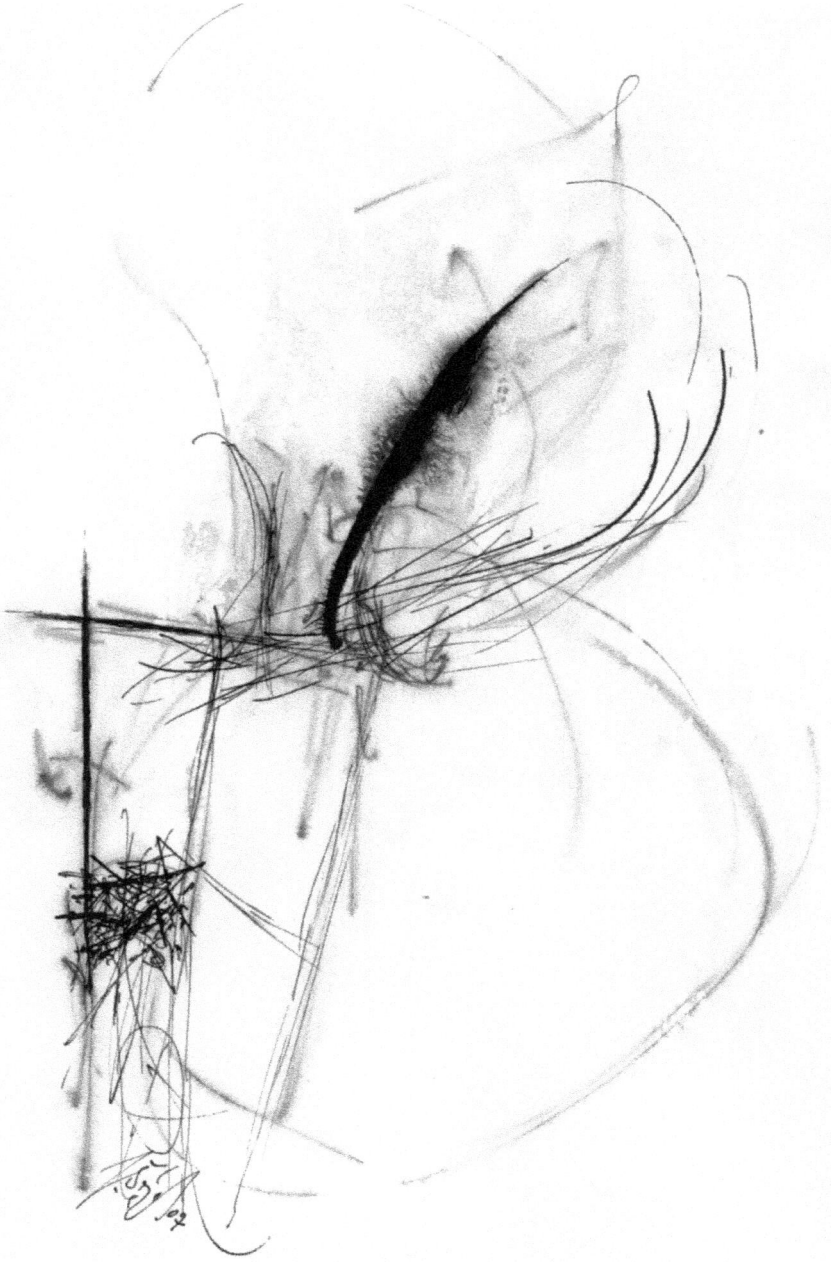

That land

1

Do you believe the green is true
of that land's periwinkle hue,
which cuts through, then takes us apart,
which does not let us stay unmarked,
where the sweet smell of rosemary
shoots to the sky in reverie,
and where ruinous treachery
discovers in me its son's tomb,
and in you the one with no womb?

You are a woman, you trust too much.
You find the truth when you misjudge.
You find what time loses the most.
You find it because you have lost.

That colourless land has no hue.
That land, with nothing but us two,
is spooning up pain like some juice
to sedate the sick and the recluse.
I am quite different from you.
I've never lost, for I've never had.

A mountain hides that unknown land,
so what we see is almost nil.

That land, with which I'll make you ill,
once offered to you as a drink,
that land, your splendour and your glint.
What befalls her, so sweet and mild,
abandoned like a little child
and taciturn and full of holes,
used by the sun at evening's close
to cover the moon with shadow's blinds?
That land, at the end, self-ignites.

I know, I know, it's colourless,
that land, the land of all my lands
where time's burning, but it stays cold,
in which our dreams strayed unresolved,
till taken apart to invite
as green and black and blue and white.

2

Do you believe it has no end,
that land so keen to separate?
Do you believe it has no bounds,
that it just plays with finite grounds
where the skyline finds its decline,
like a garden in evening's shine,
but just in eyes that always stray
from the one side (the side of grey?).
Do you believe that this pale land
might have started where God's feet stand,

the feet so bare, without a shoe,
close to our lips or morning's dew?

Its death is near, somewhere around.
It treads the sand without a sound,
it draws apart without a knock,
near to the heart, near to that rock,
behind which is nothing to find,
behind which colours become confined,
it gulps the brush, the canvas, all,
it swallows death, thus takes you whole.

Oh, look! It ends in this soft soil,
from which flowers slowly uncoil
and look around their homely land,
sickly from springs, quite pale and spent
by green and black and blue and white,
which changed to be completely right,
and soon turns pink like flamingo birds.

Then quietude will guard my words.

I've met a fountain

I've met a fountain and washed from my eyes
the sleet and all that suff'ring pain.
I've met a fountain and saw my oversights
which soon shall turn to truth again.

I look at myself with more joy and flair.
I shake my coat like a dog,
sprinkling everything with awe and despair.
My loneliness sets me agog.

I've met a fountain and we talked a lot,
more than people would ever try.
Later, when leaving this baptismal font,
I gave to geese my widest smile.

Poem of new glory

The one who comes, I applaud for his march.
I want to be his thirst, the snow in his avalanche.
The one who comes, I applaud for his march.

Down to the earth, men, hear it from within,
the boom of steps, the tree, that daring poem of green,
and rivers, with estuaries unseen.

Take a small branch, with buds just coming out,
it changes into a torch, a flame ready to sprout
and full of light, with no need to ignite.

A waterfall surges, your beaming faith
spurts up from your heart beyond thought close, intense,
whistling to the one who comes a hymn of grace.

Oh you pale and frail and brotherly and crisp.
Oh you firm, unequalled and clear like amethysts,
we are set for the month of falling leaves.

In you will we fall, in you all concludes,
we've learned of rocks, of pure springs, deep in the
                                                woods,
and of cruel courage of lonely moods.

We've learned of death, we'll deny it with thee,
and our pain, that painful drill for hope to be seen,
we put into your hands with sympathy.

And our love knows that you, so calm and bright,
will employ great rhythm and rhyme in our holy fight,
after you stripped all souls with great insight.

The one who comes, I applaud for his march.
I want to be his thirst, the snow in his avalanche.
The one who comes, I applaud for his march.

A lost soldier

A cloud, a bloodthirsty cloud,
like a horse, no saddle to mount,
floats over all the battlefields,
where someone gathered, yet soon yields.

At the far end, a little lad,
no legs, no lips, with just one hand
is chopping up some dirty lime,
drinking from the pool, full of grime.

There was a sweep of wounds and flesh.
The eve shakes down vague scents afresh
to all tucked down up to their ears.
The linden lanes, they have no trees!

The one afar can smell and lick.
From heel to head an acrostic
of the last sighs that always claim
the world that lives and has a name.

A bee flies in with a sad buzz.
No flowers to hold in someone's arms,
only a chest waits for a sting,
the chest that lets no warm love in.

He's dead, my God. He also waits
for you to sweep him to Eden's gates,
when bugles blow in vibrant boom
to silence death, to end life's doom.

He's dead, just dirt of skin that's not,
the dirt that shows us what's a blot,
which, one day, goes to fetch its staff
as far as the vale of Josafat.

There, banging its bones on hard rocks,
already close to gates' padlocks,
it will ornate the void with frills
to hide the face of future thrills.

This will stifle all memory.
This will erase all reverie
and will shake from eternal wails
under the well-earned cat- o'-nine-tails.

To whom do I belong?

To whom do I belong?

I belong to fences and sleet,
and to grasses, weathered by rains,
to clear songs, which no warbles meet,
and to desire that remains.

To whom do I belong?

I belong to things, plump and slouched,
which never met any hard edge,
I belong to pets, sad and grouched,
and to the cloud, torn on its ledge.

To whom do I belong?

I belong to fear, its grasp tight
with its fingers quite transparent,
to a bunny in a dim light,
to test its sense of smell, it went.

To whom do I belong?

I belong to the winter's grip
on fruit and death on time's own terms,
I belong to the love I let slip.
I'm an apple at the mercy of worms.

The unborn one

Past a sparkling land, where he feels at home,
his neck bent down whereto he sews and weaves,
where oft he counts what will and what won't roam,
through moist and cold, he sees flowers and leaves.

He sleeps, then doesn't, flows through all that's far,
he may have a dream and wake up afraid,
he grasps for the light of a smiling star,
at an unseen night, a night of suede.

How sweetly he wafts over endless fields!
In those graceful groves, where lovers embrace,
he opens letters with half-written leaves,
where the words *I love* tips the pans of scales.

How sweetly rolled up, like a little ball!
He waits (not knowing) for a whistling fife
to entwine him, give him thin lids and call
for a brief moment, the moment of life.

And then he'll live and then again he'll die,
and far ahead, he will wake up anew,
grasping for the light of his mother's smile
and her unseen love, her love azure blue.

The unwritten one

Put on your coat, so you won't be chilled through,
and close your eyes to lose me from your view
in such bad weather, because I come late.

Oh, those whites of my eyes begrimed with blood,
those sun-downs, whose sun I nipped in the bud
with much more cruel breakdowns of my fate.

And she, simple and never written on,
she, who knew well, the mother of my dawn,
with tears, not with verses, she starts to moan.

I talked with words, so words should calm my strife.
They stole my faith, yet brought me back my life.
Forgive them and let's go on!

Wild radish

You lead me down the leas, arrows can't hurt,
they will fly high, very high they will boom,
along full slopes, where round little clouds spurt
with wilted dandelions, long past their bloom.

Are they God's or no one's, as is the earth,
where poverty flaunts from woeful stubble-fields?
They wait for the wind, its wild soughing breath,
which scatters spores away from sandy hills.

You lead me down the leas, stretched in wide flairs
like gypsy women, soiled and ebony,
they are like brocade, like little brown hares,
like the tree's music, the ninth symphony.

Are they yours? Oh yes! You gave them to me.
You, through which I walked on my pilgrimage.
I've turned wild! Tame me! Sooth my agony!
You, in spikes of grass, wilting wild radish.

The first poem

In the memory of spilt milk,
of swifts and pines and speaking tongues,
of bread that never overeats,
of anger my silence always keeps,
straight up, my book, your spine of silk,
and breathe in full to fill your lungs.

Take me with you and let me breathe
a little longer than I'll live,
talk about freedom to your kids,
about pure water at your lips,
where, on the leas, the locusts sheathe
sun that meadows would like to sieve.

At thin-skimmed pace, I walk around
fences, rivers, this and that spot
where many hard words always hurt,
where I put on a leaden skirt,
then dive into a stony ground
to let you undo this taut knot.

I hope someone will come alone
with salvation up to his rim.
The periwinkle sleeps, its colour
protects my sunset from discolour.
I stay for ever at my birth's home,

there is my land, there is my dream.

There the world ends. There it begins.
There storms sharpen their stormy voice
till it rises and yields a song,
while death prompts it to remain strong.
The periwinkle always wins,
when singing to let life rejoice.

In the memory of spilt milk
from rocks to jugs to speaking tongues,
in the memory of the lash,
which flagellates my tender flesh,
straight up, my book, your spine of silk,
and breathe in full to fill your lungs.

Sunset

Death takes off its helmet, puts it away,
and wipes sweat off its snoot,
then plants the rifle deep into soft clay.
Let it bear fruit!

Oh you, sad crop, taking an ample soak,
who will gather your fruit?
On a huntsman's watch, a hideous cock
crows for a wilful loot,

and tears my peace, leading it to shame
through the mud and spasm, in disgrace.
You, evening gardens, like murders aflame!
You gardens of a safe place!

A summer poem

It's summer on my palette.
Ah, verses from times gone,
each line, a smiling hamlet
with kindling to keep warm.

A bitter ring hangs heavy,
is this the way to meet?
It's turning topsy-turvy,
God made it infinite,

as He does with the pebbles
in brooks, as one can hear.
A golden harvest trembles,
but only once a year.

It's me of all the givers
that flowers have beguiled
in invisible rivers,
a mother and her child,

in sleepy inns at daybreak,
in paintings in recess,
in contempt of a mistake
that separated us.

A gulf betwixt a couple,
between thousands of men,
like fish, caught without scruple,
it tears the net again!

Oh, summer on my palette,
I, too, am burned by glow,
and will, with all I've uttered,
flame up the mast, and flow

over mountains and fevers,
over a broken cross,
so the full-stop, which shivers,
will not reduce its gloss.

Job's words are closing

For the pain of all hands not reaching out
for their caresses, give me faith.
Thy rush into the night was too abrupt.
Leave slowly, peacefully, with grace.

For the pain of the soul that had its throat
cut by bygone love, let me sleep.
Let it burn out, burn out all that I wrote,
so nothing's left for me to keep.

For the pain of all throats that had to sing
by one hurt higher, let me die;
departing slowly along its last string
in glorious flames up in the sky!

A raw youth

(after reading Dostoevsky)

You follow them out, those children of words.
And in silent gaps, behind gates and walls,
you roam around like Mr. Versilov's herds.
But there's one more nook your dreams will disclose

as known and clear. Hide yourself, you can't run
from what may resurrect your bygone truth,
when hope has been used and is gone and done,
and, horror-struck, you hear your wretched youth

finding its grave. Like Mr. Versilov,
like Mr. Versilov with tortured wings,
rising up stiffly when the fish-hunt's off,
and loopless nets remind him of blind things,

while water flowed out, embraced by the seas.
Can you hold the torch? What sets it aflame?
Russia is on fire, there burn all its fields!
To be one of its sparks? Aren't you too lame?

Let's cry! It's cold. The last one to the wheel.
You follow, but where, those children of words?
A sublime day burns both its wings and will,
then roams and roams like Mr. Versilov's herds.

A poem of hope

Crows are migrating with a swarm of snakes
and with a song that makes all devils smile.
You hunt them from your Calvary escapes.
It's quite late. Time opens the mouths of guile.

Devils settled on upturned corner-stones.
So sadly they prance, their hoofs clatt'ring up.
Where are those winters, and we, in frozen homes,
after we've emptied the last glass and cup?

My Calvary, when will your cross turn green?
I'll become its fruit, I'll become its shield,
I'll be its blood, I'll be its wife of spleen,
I'll be the sun-ray that darkness will wield.

My Calvary, Calvary of my strife,
it's hard to carry it, it's great to bring in,
while Veronica's flapping little scarf
promises a place in endless suffering.

Let sheets of rain splash down on the refuge
from my last voyage. Let storms raze the ground.
Let hills seem smaller when in a deluge.
There's still love in us, despite fear all around.

The wounded

1.
The earth has opened wide. Doctoring rains
were dripping drugs to ease what was enwreathed.
All through the night, from volcano's deep veins,
hot lava seethed.

My land! You are the fever of this earth!
Trapped in your illusions, you ask once more,
still gently, softly, for all you are worth:
Where is the sore?

2.
My soul! What calmness you show on your face!
Silence drops into pits like a dead stone,
while I, like a stray doe, have lost the place
I called my home.

I'm hitting walls, while attempting to deal
with my revenge as a painful, faithful part,
well aware that my Achilles' heel
is in my heart.

What a canary told me

You look strange behind that dire wall.
My recollections. There. Adrift.
For somewhere else. And in a drawl.
Is this your birthday gift?

But why? You're singing! Wait for me!
I may learn it. I'd like to sleep.
My mother has stopped calling me.
I fear. Silent. No beep.

Freedom, I think. Do bars await?
And you? What do you write? Adrift?
Another place for my live weight?
Is this your birthday gift?

My answer to the canary

Please, hold your tongue. And don't disturb!
It's a fly buzzing, not a chant.
Lie still, lie still. Your little spur
can't hold a coffin on a slant.

Tomorrow, I'll be twenty one.
But what is all that for your kin?
I can't give back. I can't turn down.
I feel like I'm being hemmed in.

Help me to guard all words I scrawl.
I'm like you; from the Canaries.
Don't beat so much against the wall!
I have been born for vain reprise.

The lamentations of Jeremiah

Because thy rage against me, and thy tumult, is come up
into my ears, therefore will I put my hook in thy nose,
and my bridle in thy lips, and I will turn thee back by the
way by which thou camest. Isaiah, 37, 29

Oh, my stern God, quick-tempered Lord of dread,
the song that stopped time, it's thou at whom it aims,
the time my aching feet were forced to tread,
and rove through years and fight the Universe.

There may be no void, just a heavy sleep,
which can touch women to wake them from their grief,
when death sleeps on, while wild winds roar and weep,
and cruel men are gone, to my relief.

Because of the mountain, foxes walk upon
revered, but dismal, like abandoned trees,
I read from the Book, the most prophetic one
and full of light and quietude and peace.

Thou letst clouds veil thee, the waters hide,
so as not to hear Heaven's piercing cry,
and thou hast veiled me, too, with thy dark night,
yet I must not sleep, your call may be nigh.

I always listen, but thou dost not talk.
I listen with my tears, yet I don't hear.
I listen with my lips, through lanes I walk,
with unrest and silence and with my fear.

I'm that land of Night that tasted thy wrath,
that, when buried by evil, became blind.
I'm that land of Night thy whip flogged to death,
so it lost milk for each and every child.

I'm that land of Night, thou gavest it just grit
and swamps and death and hillsides, bare and steep,
and the eye of the day, but with no lid
to cover its gloom. And mothers conceived.

And mothers conceived, and, with their sweet load,
they joined the autumn to gather its fruits,
they walked, touching the ground, and yearned and
                                                longed
for an endless start, the light of my youth.

There was no light. The light, my Lord, went out.
The sun was burned by frost, that almighty switch.
And bodies of thy men shivered with fright
and with sobs and cries, so immense and rich.

Thy face turned away, thy glare turned the same,
laughed at them to avenge their robber's keep,
and paid them back with joy and gave them a name
for each vanished son the morrow will reap.

I'm that land of Night, the bare back for thy birch,
the mother of lore, the light in my gloom.
And thou tookst it away, and wentst to search
for that old vineyard: a grave-yard in bloom!

I'm that land of Night, thy daughter, thy date,
thou spoiledst my womb, my woods, my every tree,
thou pouredst burning wine into the lake,
with paralised angels, who reached to thee.

They weakened on the way and thou didst not care
if they see thee, my Lord, wings in the mud,
they were angels, heaven-dwellers they were,
I'm that land of Night, and I must shed blood.

I bleed in silence, sinfully I weep,
it's blasphemy, I know, my head feels split,
thy clemency dies away in thy whip.
When the night came, they covered me with it.

Oh, those long walks, those endless wanderings
for tears of shame, with a measure of pain,
for flakes of freedom what a black ocean brings.
I'm that land of Night, and yours I'll remain.

I pray to the night, I pray to my past,
I pray through the sparks that soon catch fire.
Oh, once and once only, when fear won't last,
when a symphony would exhaust its ire,

when wrath tumbles down, yours, I mean, my Lord,
when thou becom'st kind, able to discern
my ache for thee, not for some royal abode.
I would die for thee and for thy realm.

The bugle of winter calls for lost flakes,
those on window panes, on plains in the snow,
the flakes of heavy words in half-iced lakes,
bent over the rift of an episode.

The bugle of spring calls in a swaying voice.
Not knowing how to blow, it holds its tongue
when frozen stiff, in a snow-drift enclosed,
as every season does, if it's too young.

The bugle of summer calls with a gleam,
it flies with women and falls behind woods,
it dreams like them, but never grips its dream,
and waits for so long that it becomes used.

The bugle of autumn. Whom does it call?
Oh, me, I knew it, from evenings to morns
it tempts my ancient fear from a wild roll
in guts after death, in fruits after worms.

With what to call, if I wanted thee near,
near to my tears and woes, thou, who arest not mine?
I call thee through snow-storms, hard and severe,
I call you like leas: sleep, wait, don't resign!

Snow storms in the void of phrases most true.

What are life's gifts? The Earth, a palm and peace?
Look, the cart that betrayal forced to move
starts to run and runs to its faithful bliss.

Oh, my stern God, quick-tempered Lord of dread,
the song that stopped time, it's thou at whom it aims,
the path my aching feet were forced to tread,
and rove through years and fight the Universe.

I'm that land of Night, the darkness of earth,
I wait for love, born from cruelty's bloom.
I wait and shake, for if light was my birth,
pain has it, too, as, in you, it must loom!

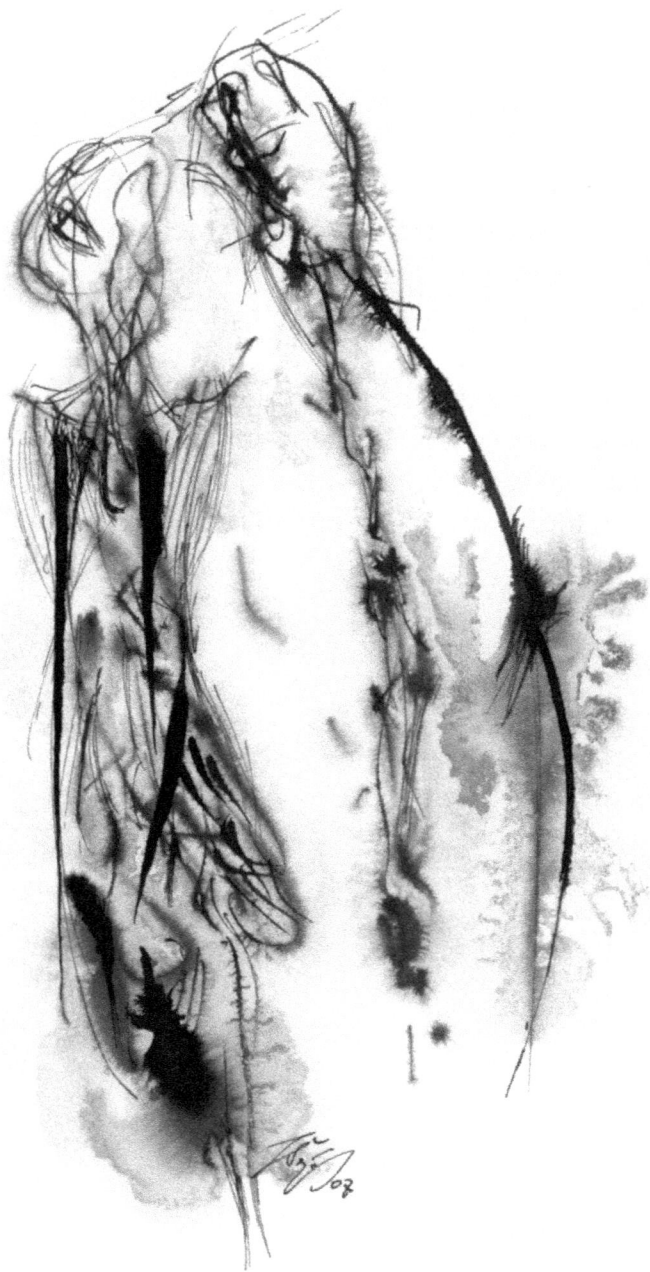

After the music

Oh, there is no void, just a heavy sleep
which can touch women to wake them from their grief,
when death sleeps on, while wild winds roar and weep,
and cruel men are gone, to my relief.

Some kind of hissing sound,
which only he could read:
the well's weep in the ground,
so immensely concealed.

He beat the time of glory, wind and void,
as if eating bread from corn never sowed.
Higher than God he was, more than of gold.

He's not bottomless, he's just not robust
for endless love, for truthful, faithful trust,
for ever and ever, the Ninth will hold...

A ride

It's late on the bridge, when train's whistle blows,
its forehead full of sparks, it may even stall
in darkness, so inexpressibly close,
and of many forms
and grim
and warts and all.

As if run over oneself on the rails,
and wine he yearned to drink was spilled on him,
his head severed, they cut out his entrails
when waiting eagerly
for Judith.
What a whim!

The first prayer

Alas! thy lips are cold …

J. W. Goethe

Not protected from my life's end,
I fall to the ground of my prayers,
a hundredfold more than I'm maimed,
I trace the pulse of my drained nerves.

Up to the pureness that has lured
my blood into a stony well,
let love for harvest be inured
up to the pureness of its hell

down to the plain with a hateful lea,
where songs are deafened by your howl,
and you must eat quite greedily
questions, too hard for your soft soul,

up to my home, an orphaned place,
being burned down up to God's eye,
who supports Heaven in reverse,
as lakes do when the sky is high.

It's warm with you

It's warm with you; it would be such a sleep.
I'd love to dive into your dusty tract.
The pity of rains would silently strip
nude carnal desire off that wretched act.

Going blind into light, in songs enclosed,
my palate feels a velvety loneliness,
it makes me drunk, then calls for a brief pause,
so not to be scared, but tuned as one piece.

To die, my father, close to nobody,
to hear no lash, no thought, no sense of touch,
to die and lie in detached rhapsody,
for ever ready, done, becoming as such.

To have at least what's the most true, to earn
my unchained void, to dream of sure decline
into nice pieces, be more taciturn,
straight in the midst, like a garden, like time.

To be dead for women, dead for my friends,
dead for my fears, dead for all who are dead.
Yes! To be just like that, with no loose ends,
and see nothing that's called a leafy spread.

It's so warm with you; what a lovely sleep.
I'd love so much to dive into your dust.
The pity of rains would silently strip
my happiness of unrequited lust.

The second prayer

So much torment beats around without end
in mankind's defenceless abodes,
and you, my God, grasp them with cruel hand,
which has no blood, no veins, no bones.

I've thought of beautiful beasts without pause.
Well, I felt I had feelings, too,
when swindled of an everlasting dose,
to which I didn't pay tribute.

To be a draught-horse rather, who always pulls
its unsweetened burden alone,
to sniff the truth, where something surely lulls,
and one is pleading: throw the stone!

To be your apple, in which cosmos bites
and munches virile worms like lard;
your apple from intoxicating piles
of mothers, tears, stars and the Bard.

An apple of freedom on a sagged branch,
a brilliant fruit from winter harvest,
so that your cruel hand, my Lord, can't touch
the fragile things my heart has harnessed.

Red painting

What's dying here? The voice of bells was bright
but sad, as it quietly bloomed and rolled,
and blossomed and flowered with painful blight.
Its name is pietà, that's how it's called.

Flowers from apple trees, like snow with scent,
showered upon girls in daybreak's light;
someone took cracked glass and started to paint
autumnal breasts and worlds, enlarged and bright.

I'm lost in words – it's the motion of death
I'd love to sew on the buttons of God,
and let Him smell from true flowery beds,
and drink from the wound when bleeding has stopped.

In summer time, rich breakfasts on lawns,
some fruit and meat, and mouths full of food.
In the time of spoil, with no pleasant morns,
I want a painting in which berries look good!

Wild women (I hope they won't see me, tell)
shall run, naked, to satisfy their lust,
to catch the high chaser, who shoots so well
in endless pools, with continuing thrust.

Then I'll return, the bells will sound so bright,
but sad, when they quietly bloom and roll,
and blossom and flower with painful blight,
with the name of pietà, that's my call.

A lea

She's still young, she can hardly know
that she's only just turning green.
I want to go and watch her grow,
lying with her, as I have been.

She's not responding, feels so cold,
as if the lea turned into stone.
Oh, where's the stitch, what seams were sewed?
Where is the note of the last tone?

Someone's grazing, someone's allowed.
I go around, I'm at the edge.
My long lost love, don't blame me loud!
Riper and firmer I'll emerge.

The Christmas poem

The sadness of fêtes, chorals, windows, lights
and children's eyes, wide open with great wonder.
My driftwood, tell, how stale became bread bites
when crusty pleasures had been torn asunder?

Our mouths turned death into liquid whey,
nothing belonged to us from concert halls.
Horses are cold, harnessed to a fast sleigh,
they want to go and break through snowy walls.

Let's end the liturgy! We've prayed enough,
enough we've burned in Him, to no avail,
till we fell down like a poor epitaph
for lonely holes, where all our dreams turned stale.

The church calms the organ and grows arcane
where our faith shone so bright not long ago.
My driftwood, tell me, where'll you change your train,
when the point is reached with nowhere to go?

The third elegy

I dream of longing. I know it will pass
before I wake. My kingdom is the prey.
Sung, in pain, to the name that all engulfs,
I leave this sunny place to take away
my song to timeless lands of no true deed,
where bare hearts have to wrest with their dark lore,
where, woe to us, what tempts must soon recede,
where fall and abyss can be rhymed no more.

More than autumnal was the hair I stroked,
more than sad dreams, like rivers full of tears,
more vernal than an avenue, evoked
by a chest chasing the most beautiful spheres,
like dawns, too young but snowing winterly,
are arms and slopes of hips in steep descent,
this womb is God's grove, blessed and summerly,
made fertile by Cramp's brush, wresting with paint.
But why did he remove it from its stand,
and tore the white, and mixed all colours thus,
and gave it to the wind to re-create?
Why does he rub hot salves in evil's guts?

Girls sleep in their beds. Who spreads their sheets?
Who pierces sweet circles, their shame amidst?
And brings them tears and loves them and deceives?
Who plays with fate for cruel memories?

Who tears them from their land, creating that slit
which, not long after, despair would fill up?
Who is so hungry that, not yet replete,
grows them much stronger, both fertile and ripe?

Who, if not He, who used to instruct Rolle,
that drunken angel, to race for every inn,
and poured, through his pure mouth into his soul,
strong poison to torture the saint in him.
Who, if not He, who lets our urge be stirred
for endless flow, wine of the multitude,
who bears us, just as long as we are hurt,
and ties us to the earth in ill-repute.
Who, if not He, so much beloved by those
poor soldiers, for whom a night's lullaby
was heaven's come-down, moving even stones?
He, who always creates, while standing by!

Oh, there's no solitude! Here no one loves!
Girls sleep in their beds and the beds lie!
He enters, loads them, with flame engulfs
for an odd prayer, abysmal and blind,
He unties all straps and opens every niche,
He quenches your thirst with a burning grief,
He sacks your sore soul, so it has no wish
but to forget its dream. And that's called relief …

There was a ferryman. In a bridgeless land,
bringing wayfarers to the other shore.
He had a house and a firm ship. Each hand,
he used to say, grows in the stream with each oar.

Those who don't come back, what do they know of him!
What can he know of them, with no stop, no stay!
Just as he was, they saw him as a whim.
Just that they had to come and float away.

You also came. Thousands more will pass through.
Ask for nothing. Just be led across.
And pay your fare. Be silent. Don't pursue
the true face of your aged and painful loss.
You'll be there soon and the ship will return.
You'll march forward, fooled by what's left behind.
Something awaits you. It's late for death's turn.
Spies of the horizon call: the day is nigh.

The third prayer

My bones turned stiff, as it says in the Book.
All night I have been staying at this place
and prayed to you and to you I called: look!
All night long my grief blossomed on my face.

Here harlots dragged, observing me askance,
grown fat by loneliness, they asked me: come
and sleep with us – but I made no advance,
with shackles on, my shame remained all numb.

What could I give to them, what could I say,
keen to grow into your heavenly void,
and the growth was pointless, to no avail,
it pressed me to the ground, where all was soiled.

My Lord, those tears and all in gloom!
Look at my naked faith – it has no leaves!
In your compassion, can't you find some room
for a poor psalmist to rest there in peace?

Girl's song

Hold on, you two, I have just tripped,
the shouting voice, that's only wind,
which reaches everywhere and spies.
Stay put, you two, and mind your eyes.
The first one – all my thanks are his –
he may hide in my tenderness.
The second one – from bedside edge
will launch his love to my love's surge …

Winter has passed. I let my dreams
enter me with most risky schemes.
With you, my first, I'll sit all night,
and wake you up when day is light.
Comb me, my second, I am ripe,
then pierce me, you're my archetype.
Let's clatter down in our coach,
to flow and find that springtime's brooch,
like tears, when giving myself up.
My dear, keep combing, I am ripe.

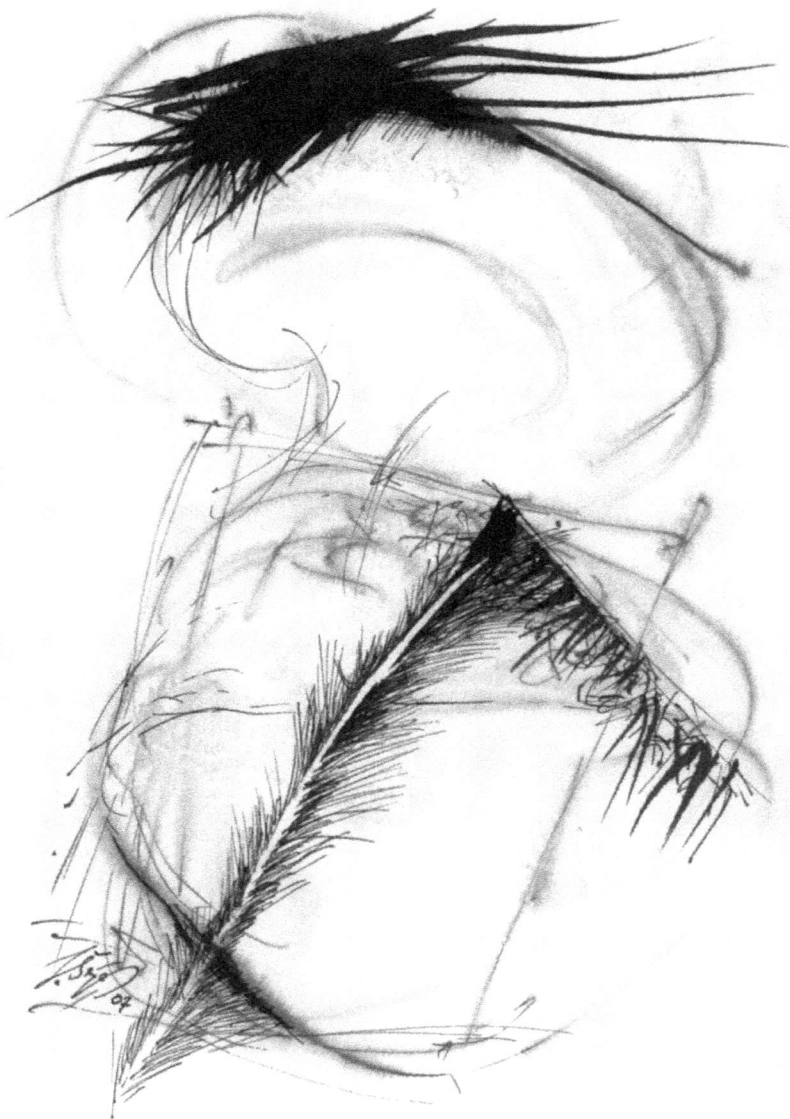

The seventh elegy

I write to you, Karin. Are you alive,
or already where longing cannot thrive,
and those wild years of yours will no more rave?
Then ask the name on the stone of your grave
to ease its weight. My lady, ask the roses
to close their heads. Ask all that decomposes
to read to you about my own demise.
My verse mutes death, so I face you with ease,
cruelly young and, for the first time, grown;
my youth looks like a king who lost his crown.
You must have known how short of wings we were
not to tempt rising in an angelic flair,
how blood filled our laughs, our tears and our sense!
At last, I've found my fall, and tell you whence.

Once up in heaven (by this I mean God)
my lucid view, struck by a lightning bolt,
was bleeding and bled before it set down.
It was a dream, recalling everyone:
my mother, father, brothers and my home,
it was a dream where one feels like the foam
floating on water between spreading rings,
it was a dream of lunar mirrorings.
If I didn't awake, then why that dream?
Why was I left in such an icy stream?
The fall of God! The boy is on his own,

without that blissful might that had pulled down
all hurdles, and moved near what was far, and kept
Hell closed by the scent of a violet.
The boy is then alone and wakes spellbound
to a real, evil world. What has he found?

Time is a charlatan, not keen to heal.

Yet once, my fall seemed to be staying still,
suddenly stopped by Narcissa's embrace.
All hovered and, with unspeakable grace,
talked about happiness. It was that tongue
no wind can blow away, however strong,
that mother language of lips and hands and eyes,
of finding rest between two beloved thighs,
the tongue of safe refuge in thrilling joy,
that special tongue that does not need to toy.
What did Narcissa want from a looking glass,
if all she ever touched turned into ice?
As Narcissus, her shade, she wished nothing more
but to see herself with no soul, no form
in that transparent screen; she gathered words
about hard beauty, only diamonds can trace;
she yearned to learn her place in people's dreams.
She was no source. She was drowning in streams.

Whence does it gush out to flush us away?
Whose sleepless nights have covered mine to stay,
then burgeoned out through all heavenly spheres?
I have found my fall. And where? In my tears!

My tears were falling down on muddy trails,
falling for the live realm of groans and wails,
their fall so shameless, I write to you, Karin,
please plead with the stone I'm washing with rain.
I feel like rain falling upon your tomb,
like falling tears, timeless, losing all plume.
Please read this, Karin, if you are alive,
and not already where longing can't thrive,
and those wild years of yours can find no bliss.

I know a girl, as small as a kiss,
hiding in her mouth, not yet allowed out,
stretching in the sun, half behind a cloud,
so as not to burn, but fall asleep with ease.
She's as young as Earth, as light as a breeze,
as early foliage, as dawn, as happiness.
I know nice days, too. Yet these just gave me less.

You knew it well, Karin! Do you know still?
I know great women, too: mothers in fear
for their sad sons they may never see.
I know my land, too; what an ecstasy!
And trust? I know, but where to find it, where?
I know awakenings from pain and despair –
and it helps not to know, it helps not to fret
about betrayal when one can't forget.

My verse mutes death. See! I still dream and hide
what storms it screens, what horrors may abide.
What will we grasp? What stays there permanent?
What dies there, too? What falls find there no end?

Lovers? –
        I didn't want to say a word,
please forgive Narcissa her sins, her world
and light a candle and pray for this Earth here.
Don't allow December to be severe;
let April give it what flowers may need.
The night be its banner to flaunt, to lead
into the world, when time is ripe for stars.
Let lovers laud it for their pain and scars.

So cruelly young and, for the first time, grown;
my laugh spills blood, my tears are bleeding down,
abandoned by God, forsaking God's love,
I write to you Karin, not sure if I'm alive.

The eighth elegy

Rain against the sun,
where are we to hide
when this rainbow's arch
wants us to feel hurt?
Old paintings' dimmed shine
shows them glorified,
while tailors of hues
tie the broken thread.

The quay is aflame,
and my hidden stream
escalates my thirst
with each single splash.
I won't drink at all
from this stripped off dream.
It mustn't turn nude,
even in distress!

I dream of a stag
in cruel rutting time;
he denied what's closed,
once roused and aflame.
When out of the woods,
he changed to a shrine:
Couldn't he be shot?
Couldn't he be slain?

When any carcass,
any beast of prey
loses its foothold,
where does it sink, where?
Whatever its bed,
alone it must stay,
illuminated
by its vain despair.

Why does much blood run
back to its old state,
into its mother,
a calm river bed?
It feels no trauma
when they operate;
in burial grounds,
they find no one dead.

I feel such tenderness
that still stays with me
from old bygone times,
when I try to trace
the colour of gloom
in the agony
of my darkened soul,
where love finds no place.

Rain against the sun,
that's always the start.
It remains to find
just some modest end.
The rainbow, you saw
as your lover's heart,
and, in faith, you wished
all would stay unchanged,

It was no rainbow
you found when arrived,
some dilettante
smeared its radiance.
She was not alone.
She was with her child,
as if grief could have
fathered its presence,

as if its newborn,
being abandoned
(I mean your love, yes)
had found its way back
to pre-conception,
from which you'll be born
only by death now
in your dreamed out world,

the world of your verse,
the shore of your sea,
in the darkened flow,
an island of light,
in the soil of faith,
dreamed out modesty,
the joy not to be
inside you, my life.

So many paintings
collect dust in stores!
So many palettes
the brush has not met!
So much desire
of an untouched source!
Oh, my maestro,
your model is dead!

And I still don't know,
at this late night hour,
whether death's image,
I see in my dream,
reaches to the sky
into which I tower,
or if I'll reach, too,
its grace and esteem.

A hangover

My lament, may I call you, moan?
Would you mind joining me to bemoan?

And scent – to smell you is a bliss.
I love to breathe in your malice.

So many curtains hang apart!
I feel much pain in lungs and heart.

It must've been due to many drinks.
It must've been because of my kinks.

In due course, all believe in diet.
I'm strong, each dinner is my fiat.

I'm hungry! So what! I shall eat
my tears and fears, my hateful feat.

I'm thirsty, too, I'll drink some ale
with downpours, storms, with icy hail,

and then, worn out, I fall asleep,
leaving my couplet incomplete.

My lament, why tell I'm alone?
Would you then join me in my moan?

Night and day

Dead tired I've been, carting hay;
dry as a bone on this warm day,
and down so many roads.
I'm just a black horse, but I feel
that I won't sleep, unless I steal
something of windy blows.

I'll dive in darkness, as they said,
and this is what I oft regret,
feeling my tingling hoofs.
I'll have a sip from the dark night,
and change my coat from black to white.
Look! It's dawn above roofs!

The moist one

At night, the forest hears you well, my love:
your humming in trees, your teardrops on leaves,
your gentle hand, obscured in dawn's dew glove,
touching the nests, as warm as your skin feels.

You are still shivering when you declaim
my verses to brooks, blushful in your breath
on arms and breasts. I wait for the same,
as my words harden my lips to dry earth.

You don't, you cannot know what has been said,
that, with your name on my lips, I often wept,
that I have you like woods, like the dusk of day,

lengthening to bring the absent one near.
I know I'll wake, my dreams wipe their eyes clear,
and thus restored, I rise from my decay.

Autumn

Autumn is already
stripping summer days;
I am still not ready
to move from this place.

Your windstorms, oh summer,
will drive you insane!
Oh God, so much hunger
and torment and pain

eat my guts like vermin,
while wind blows from hills
pestilence and famine
on us – stubble-fields.

Who will take us over,
wretched body and soul?
Be quiet! In October
time will buckle low.

My trees of years

My trees of years, how do you grow?
From the first or hundredth sight, I know
that you are watered just by tears,
and therefore wood is your premise
to start fire with glare and flare;
then half blind eyes become aware
that it's you who's been set ablaze.
My trees, my trees, so old, yet crazed!

There were wild beasts lurking in you,
it was your lion-tamer's woo
that deprived me of happiness.
All that I had has become his.
The water gushes from your spring,
the dawn rises when your birds sing,
the sun sets down into your trust.
My trees, your rings are full of rust!

Ah, a bit longer, let me look
sky up, where heaven has unhooked
its most reddened hue in the east.
Let's celebrate, let's have a feast,
let freedom serve some wine, then sway,
let not my bed be gnawed away
by what I wished to sew up clear
with my second and twice tenth year!

Translator's Note

When walking the streets of Prague (or any other Czech town), one can stop the passers by and mention the name Jiří Orten, and about one in five will immediately start reciting "I write to you Karin", or long passages from "That Land", or many of his other poems.

Why is his poetry so memorable? I suspect it is because Orten wrote in rhyme, with a strict rhythm, just as we see in more than 95% of his poems.

I became so obsessed with his rhyme and rhythm that I undertook the difficult task of translating his poetry into English – a very different language – so that readers from other countries could experience the same fascination with his style as most of his compatriots do.

My guide was based on two simple thoughts: 1) How would Orten have written his poems if his tool of expression had been English rather than Czech? 2) How would he employed rhyme and rhythm if, instead of having Czech poets, French impressionists and symbolists in his background, he had read Shakespeare, Byron, Keats, Barrett-Browning, Eliot, all of whom used rhyming with iambic rhythm?

It is up to the readers of English to judge whether I have succeeded or not. If only a few of you carry some of

Orten's poems in your heads, then I shall be fully satisfied.

Josef Tomáš